IT STARTS WITH ONE

IGNITING THE PASSION FOR THE MISSION OF THE CHURCH

Seacoast Church

THOMAS

Since

NASHVILLE   DALLAS   MEXICO CITY   RIO DE JANEIRO

Published in Nashville, Tennessee, by Thomas Nelson. Thomas Nelson is a registered trademark of Thomas Nelson, Inc.

Thomas Nelson, Inc., titles may be purchased in bulk for educational, business, fund-raising, or sales promotional use. For information, please e-mail SpecialMarkets@ThomasNelson.com.

It Starts with One: Igniting the Passion for the Mission of the Church

ISBN: 978-1-41854-613-7

Printed in the United States of America

11 12 13 14 15 QG 5 4 3 2 1

It all started with one:
The holy one
who descended from heaven,
gave us new life,
and returned to heaven.
The story is not finished.
It's just beginning.
It starts with one.

[**CONTENTS**]

[INTRODUCTION]

Resurrection Power

Geoff Surratt

In 1939 three men, led by Albert Einstein, approached the president of the United States with the secret to the power of chain reactions. Their work became known as the Manhattan Project, and the chain reaction led to the atomic bomb. Equally powerful, although in a different way, is the power of the truth of the gospel. When Jesus appeared *alive* to his disciples, history changed forever. How do we handle the kind of information that will change history? We're going to look at the beginning of the church in Acts for the next six weeks, and we'll see how those early Christians took the gospel message and used it to change the world.

The disciples knew that what set Jesus apart was the mystery and power of his resurrection. He'd fed the five thousand on a hillside in Judea—a remarkable miracle. But Elijah had fed a widow and her son with the same cup of grain for a month. Jesus had turned the water into wine, but Moses had parted the Red Sea so the Israelites could escape slavery in Egypt. And Jesus had raised men from the dead, but so did Paul, when a particularly long sermon led a young man to fall out of a window to his death. But no one in history had ever risen from the dead of his own power.

That single action proved for all time that Jesus was, in fact, the Christ. He was God.

For the disciples, knowing Jesus this way meant that God was no longer simply a concept, a "higher power" to be respected but not known. Jesus entered their homes and their lives, he taught them about his kingdom, and he prepared them to minister in his name for the ages to come. And they knew then that everything they'd learned—all of the Old Testament and Jesus' whole earthly ministry—was all leading up to this moment when he rose from the dead. Acts is the pivotal point of the Bible, the time when the lessons became actions and the power of the Holy Spirit came to rest on God's people. Pentecost is the Manhattan Project of Christianity. When the Holy Spirit was unleashed, the small Jewish sect grew to become a movement of thousands of people across the entire known world.

There are three things we want you to know as you go through this study. First, God is real. We see this in the resurrection and we know it to be true because Christ lives. Second, we can tap into the power of the resurrection—it is available to us as God's children. And finally, we access this power by seeking God with all our hearts. In Jeremiah 29:13 we read, "You will seek me and find me when you seek me with all your heart."

Stop pretending you have it all together, and confess your brokenness to God. Ask him to be Lord of your life—all the messy details of it—and refuse to budge until you experience the resurrection power of Christ. It will heal and inspire as you make your way through life in a fallen world. And it will give you access to the wonderful community of believers who support one another until that day Christ returns to call us home.

There is power, wonder-working power, in the blood of the Lamb. Are you willing to make it yours?

[HOW TO USE
   THIS GUIDE]

Each session in this guide includes the following elements:

Consider

In this study you'll discuss Acts 1–6 in depth, with each session focusing on a different topic in the chapter. You'll start off by reading a short introduction to the topic.

Read

This section is designed to help you go into a deeper study time. You will read a selected passage from Scripture, making notes of what stood out to you in the text. This is a time to go into the Word and prayerfully consider what God is telling you in these verses. Questions will be available to assist you with your observations of the passage. All Scripture passages referenced in this study are from the New International Version (NIV), unless otherwise noted.

Reflect

The reflection questions in each section will challenge you to look deeper into how the topic relates to you. This is a time of learning from God and learning about yourself and others.

Action Steps

This section provides practical suggestions to help you live out the truths you learn in the study.

Group Discussion/Youth Discussion/Family Discussion

Our hope is that you'll come together with other individuals, couples, your family, a small group, or a youth group and experience this journey in community. You'll watch the five-minute DVD introduction at the start of your meeting and then dive into these questions for discussion. These discussion questions will help you get conversation started.

Notes

This is a place for you to record your insights and observations throughout your study. In addition, you may want to purchase a separate notebook or journal for some extended journaling on the topics in this study.

Additional Resources

If you're still thirsty for more teaching, you can visit the It Starts with One website at www.mystartswithoneresources.com. There you'll find resources for further study, sermon notes, and promotional materials for your church to use so that your entire congregation can be aligned in learning these truths together—from your pastor to your adult ministries all the way down to youth and children. There's something for everyone.

CHANGING YOUR WORLD

"But you will receive power when the Holy Spirit comes on you; and you will be my witnesses in Jerusalem, and in all Judea and Samaria, and to the ends of the earth."

—Acts 1:8

[**CONSIDER**]

CHANGING YOUR WORLD

By Greg Surratt

Have you ever wondered if your life is really making a difference? It's something we all think of from time to time, and the question is rooted in a desire that was hardwired in us by our Creator. We are the church, and the Holy Spirit has empowered us with the job of spreading God's kingdom here on earth. So what are we going to do about it?

Jesus was the original difference maker. Two thousand years ago he came to live, teach, die, and rise again. The world was broken, but Christ came to make it whole. And part of his plan is to spread the news of his kingdom through each one of us. And we can learn how to be effective by watching his life and ministry.

In Acts 1:4 Jesus told his disciples, "Do not leave Jerusalem, but wait for the gift my Father promised, which you have heard me speak about." You can practically see the disciples frantically running around and making plans the minute they heard the command to share the good news with all the world. But Christ told them to hang on. Slow down. Take a breather here, and be open to the voice of the Lord. They knew what he was talking about because they'd seen him do it previously. Before launching into a mission, Jesus always took time to hear from God. When the time came to start his earthly ministry, Jesus went into the wilderness for a forty-day time-out. And when he was approaching the cross, he took a time-out in the Garden of Gethsemane. Jesus knows we need a time-out when the world's coming at us too fast and we don't understand things. When you take the time to focus and to listen for God's voice, you'll gain perspective.

Another reason Jesus asked the disciples to wait was because they needed to receive all God had to offer them. The same goes for you. God does not intend for you to go it alone in the battle for his kingdom. He has powerful tools for you to use, and the most

important one is the gift of the Holy Spirit. Jesus commanded his disciples to wait, to take a time-out, for the gift his Father promised. Then he said, "For John [the Baptist] baptized with water, but in a few days you will be baptized with the Holy Spirit" (Acts 1:5). The Holy Spirit is God's presence within you as a believer. You'll find that there are times when a message will pop in your head, and that will be the voice of the Holy Spirit. There will be times when the world is standing against you, and the Holy Spirit will give you the words to say and the courage to stand. And there will be times when you are sad, your heart will mourn, and the Holy Spirit will be there to comfort you. The Holy Spirit's work on earth is what changes lives and extends God's kingdom.

But you cannot tap into this power without focus. You must train your attention on your mission. We see in Acts 1 that the disciples were immediately distracted from their mission to make more disciples of Christ. Instead they turned to him and said, "Is now the time you're going to conquer the Romans?" At this point their vision was too small, for God had plans much greater than just freedom from the rule of the Roman Empire. We, too, need to know that the time of the Lord's favor has come, but instead of spreading this good news, some of us are arguing about the color of the carpet or the style of music we use in worship. There are more important issues in the world—poverty, hunger, abuse, death, and loneliness. We could be addressing all of these things if we'd just focus on Christ's mission for us.

If we don't expect to be used by God, we won't be. William Carey, the great missionary, said, "Expect great things from God and attempt great things for God." God has a mission for you somewhere; do you know what it is? It could be in your very own home, in your neighborhood, in your city, or at the ends of the earth. But if you don't expect to be used, you'll never see the greatness God wants to accomplish through you for his kingdom.

[**READ**]

Begin by reading through the entirety of Acts 1. Commit to reading it through every day this week.

Memory Verse

"But you will receive power when the Holy Spirit comes on you; and you will be my witnesses in Jerusalem, and in all Judea and Samaria, and to the ends of the earth."
(Acts 1:8)

Acts 1:1–11

1. According to Acts 1:1–3, what was the purpose of the gospel of Luke? Compare these verses to Luke 1:1–4.

2. Jesus told the disciples to wait for the promised Holy Spirit. Do you think the disciples knew what this meant? Do you know?

3. In Acts 1:6, the disciples showed that they still didn't totally understand Jesus' mission. They were still expecting Jesus to reign in an earthly kingdom. In response, Jesus gave them a mission. According to verse 8, what is this mission?

4. Sum up the events that take place in Acts 1:1–11. Try to put yourself in the disciples' place. What do you think they felt and experienced?

Acts 1:12–26

1. According to verses 13–14, what did the disciples do while waiting for the fulfillment of Jesus' promise?

2. List the eleven apostles. Who had been the twelfth? What happened to him?

3. How do verses 21–22 define "an apostle"?

For Further Study, Read and study Luke 24, which tells of Jesus' resurrection and ascension.

[**REFLECT**]

- How would you define your mission as a follower of Christ?

- Reread Acts 1:8. Would someone observing your life say that this describes you? Why or why not?

- What, if anything, keeps you from being fully passionate about being Jesus' witness?

- Is there anybody in your life to whom you feel God is specifically calling you to be a witness?

[ACTION STEPS]

⮑ This week, share with at least one person about what Jesus Christ means to you or something he has done in your life. Commit to doing this each week, at least through the remainder of the Acts study. For help, as you read through Acts, make a note of the various ways the disciples witness to others about Jesus.

⮑ As we saw in Acts 1:13–14, the disciples relied heavily upon prayer. Whatever your prayer life looks like, take it to the next level this week. If you don't pray, commit to praying five minutes each day. If you already pray regularly, try a new method, such as writing out your prayers in a journal.

⮑ Not only did the disciples devote themselves to prayer, but they did this with a group of other believers. Find a group of Christians with whom you can gather regularly for prayer.

⮑ What is keeping you from living out the mission Jesus gave in Acts 1:8? Make a list of your priorities—the things that are important to you as well as what takes up most of your time. Where does your focus on Jesus and his mission fall? How can you realign your priorities?

[GROUP DISCUSSION]

The following questions are meant to help your group enter into meaningful discussion that we pray will help you become more fully devoted followers of Christ. They are simply a guide, so you don't have to use or get through all of them. You may want to look through them ahead of time and identify the ones that would work well with your group. Any questions you don't get to might be used by your group members for study and reflection in their personal devotional times. And if your group is already comfortable together, feel free to skip the icebreaker question. Remember, it's all about community, so let the Spirit guide your discussion where he wants it to go.

ICE BREAKER

If you were to go live on a deserted island and could carry only one thing with you, what would it be?

Reflections from the Week

Depending on your group size, break into groups of two or three and do or ask the following:

- Have everyone review their notes from their personal study time. Share with one another what you learned from the readings. Are there any questions you'd like to discuss with the group?

- What are your expectations for yourself during this study? How would you like to see yourself grow?

- As a group, discuss what steps you can take to challenge one another to use this study as you seek to grow.

[] **Session 1**

➲ *Discussion Questions*

Read Acts 1:1–11.

- Summarize the events that occur in this passage.

- How do you imagine the disciples were thinking and feeling after these events?

- Do you ever relate to this in your own relationship with God?

Read Acts 1:8 and Matthew 28:19–20.

- What mission did Jesus leave with his disciples?

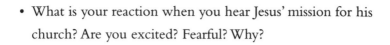

- What is your reaction when you hear Jesus' mission for his church? Are you excited? Fearful? Why?

- Would someone observing your life know that this is your mission? Why or why not?

- What is one thing you can do this week to obey Jesus' final command to his disciples?

Challenge

As a life group, practice being Jesus' witnesses with each other and within your spheres of influence. Discuss practical ways you can share the love of Christ in your relationships this week. If you feel comfortable, and if time allows, share your testimony with one another.

Close in [PRAYER]

Heavenly Father, thank you for bringing this group of brothers and sisters in you together to study your call on our lives. Clear our schedules and open our hearts to take a time-out this week to focus on you alone, for without focus we are lost in our mission. We receive the gift of your Holy Spirit with thanksgiving, and we ask that you'd use us to further your kingdom even today. Amen.

[**YOUTH DISCUSSION**]

God wants you to be a part of the team that will spread the kingdom of God to the ends of the earth. It's a huge adventure, and he has a job for you. Are you willing to take the plunge and share his good news throughout the world?

THIS SESSION'S [BIG] IDEA

Expect to be used by God!

Memory Verse

"But you will receive power when the Holy Spirit comes on you; and you will be my witnesses in Jerusalem, and in all Judea and Samaria, and to the ends of the earth." (Acts 1:8)

 **SESSION 1**

➲ *Discussion Questions*

1. Did the poem at the beginning of the video inspire you? How?

2. Why was the guy counting throughout the video?

3. It's our job as believers to spread the gospel throughout the world. What are you doing to join this mission?

4. At the end of the video, the speaker says, "There's no plan B." We're the only ones who can spread the Word of God throughout the earth. How does that make you feel?

5. What are you going to do about it?

Challenge

Share God's love with one person this week. Write down his or her name here if you know who you plan to talk to.

[FAMILY DISCUSSION]

This week's message: God will use us to share his love with the world.

[LIFEBOOK] Idea of the Week

"But you will receive power when the Holy Spirit comes on you; and you will be my witnesses in Jerusalem, and in all Judea and Samaria, and to the ends of the earth." (Acts 1:8)

Summary

God wants to use us to spread his kingdom to the ends of the earth, and he tells us how we can be a part of this exciting adventure. First, we must be patient and take time to listen to him. Second, we can receive the gift of the Holy Spirit, who will give us the power to minister for God. Third, we must focus on the mission and not get distracted by things that aren't important. And finally, we must expect God to use us!

[LIFELINE] The Main Point

God gives us the Holy Spirit so we can spread his good news to the world.

[LIFEVERSE] Memorize This!

"But you will receive power when the Holy Spirit comes on you; and you will be my witnesses in Jerusalem, and in all Judea and Samaria, and to the ends of the earth." (Acts 1:8)

[LIFECHALLENGE]

Talk together as a family.

1. Is our family too busy to hear what God wants us to do for him in our neighborhood and beyond? If so, what are some things we can cut out of our schedules?

2. What difference does God want us to make in our neighborhood?

3. How will the Holy Spirit help us do that?

4. Do you expect God to use you to further his kingdom? How?

Action

⮑ Agree on a service project you can do together this week to share God's love with those who live near you.

NOTES

RECEIVING THE GIFT

When the day of Pentecost came, they were all together in one place. Suddenly a sound like the blowing of a violent wind came from heaven and filled the whole house where they were sitting. They saw what seemed to be tongues of fire that separated and came to rest on each of them. All of them were filled with the Holy Spirit and began to speak in other tongues as the Spirit enabled them.

—Acts 2:1–4

[CONSIDER]
RECEIVING THE GIFT
By Greg Surratt

The Jewish people had come from dozens of surrounding countries to gather in Jerusalem to celebrate the Pentecost. It had been seven weeks since Christ's resurrection, and there was an energy running through them. You could hear the hum of hundreds of languages being spoken across the courtyards, when suddenly they were silenced by a loud noise that could only be the power of God.

Before this moment, God's followers had occasionally been empowered by his Spirit—Samson had superhuman strength, and David's mighty men won impossible battles. But at Pentecost, the Holy Spirit came upon Christ's followers in a new, even more powerful way. His disciples were filled with the Spirit permanently rather than temporarily, which enabled them to proclaim the gospel boldly, perform more miracles, and even to speak in tongues.

In Acts 2:4, we read that "all of them . . . began to speak in other tongues as the Spirit enabled them." This idea of speaking in tongues has divided Christians for ages, so we should take a look at what was going on that day in Jerusalem.

There are a few interpretations for what we now call "speaking in tongues." One interpretation and practice has been utilized by Christians throughout history. The early church primarily used it in their private prayer or in corporate worship, and it refers to a mystical ability to speak in another language that is *not* a known language. This was not the form of "speaking in tongues" used in this passage of Acts.

Instead, this verse uses the Greek word *glossa*, and refers to a supernatural ability to speak in another language that is a *known* language. In other words, those people who had come from their own countries and spoke their own languages—they could all understand what was happening because it was spoken in their tongue. It set the people up to be able to understand the gospel, which is always God's desire for us.

NOTES

The work of God among us should be amazing and unexplainable. If you can easily explain everything that's happening in your church, then God is probably not at work there. We should be part of his work, and as God's children, we're supposed to stand out and make a difference. Whenever there's a move of God, people will call it weird—those who are filled with God's Spirit will be considered weird too. But when you tap into the power of God in his Holy Spirit, you receive his gift, and it's an amazing and mysterious thing.

When we encounter this Spirit-filled life, the only question we can ask is, "What should we do?" We're faced with our sin and our own agendas in light of God's holiness, and we have to respond. We have to ask what our next steps will be. So, what do we do with the reality that Jesus is God?

First, repent of your sin. You can't live in harmony

with Jesus' calling if you are carrying around the burden of sin. You must turn from your own way of doing things and put your faith in Jesus Christ's death and resurrection. At the moment you ask Christ to be Lord of your life, the Holy Spirit will set up a permanent residence within you. Your next step should be to get baptized. Just as the Jews were celebrating the work of the Lord at Pentecost, so we can celebrate the fact that Christ is alive by publicly identifying with him through the ceremony of baptism. As we go through life, the Holy Spirit within us will continue to fill us to overflowing as we seek him in all our circumstances.

When we take this step, our faith will become contagious. More people will come into the body of Christ because they see his love at work in us, and they will be drawn to it. We'll commit ourselves to the fellowship of believers, and our ministry together will be led by the power of the Holy Spirit.

This is God's desire for all believers—for us to continually seek his Holy Spirit's power so that our love for God and others will grow and develop every day. Knowing this, how would you answer the fundamental question: Do I have all that God wishes for me to enjoy?

[**READ**]

Begin by reading through the entirety of Acts 2. Commit to reading it through every day this week.

NOTES

Memory Verse

All of them were filled with the Holy Spirit and began to speak in other tongues as the Spirit enabled them. (Acts 2:4)

1. Make a list of everything you learned about the Holy Spirit in Acts 2.

2. What immediate effects of the Holy Spirit do we see in Peter and the other believers in this chapter?

3. According to Acts 2:38–39, who is the Holy Spirit for?

4. Sum up the content of Peter's sermon. What caused so many people to repent and be saved?

5. Read 1 Peter 3:14–16. How did Peter illustrate this in his sermon in Acts 2?

6. Read Luke 22:54–62. How had Peter changed by the time of this sermon in Acts? What do you think had caused him to change so much in such a short period of time?

7. How does Acts 2:42–47 describe the community of believers after the Holy Spirit came?

[REFLECT]

"Hosanna, they sing hosanna. And the voices wave joy that we are the saved ones, the rescued and saved ones and who cannot wonder at the wonder of this?" —Ann Voskamp

- Would you say that the resurrection has truly had an effect on you or made a difference in your life? What evidence would you point to?

- Think through what the resurrection means or could potentially mean to the following list of people. It may help to start out your answer for each group by saying, "Because Jesus rose from the dead . . ."

— you

— your family

— your job

— your community

— the world

- Pope John Paul II once said, "Do not abandon yourselves to despair. We are the Easter people, and hallelujah is our song." What do you think it should look like to be "Easter people"? What does a resurrection life look like?

- Think about the lost friends and family you've been focused on and praying for. What are their lives like without Jesus? What difference would the resurrection make to them?

NOTES

[ACTION STEPS]

Tomb, thou shalt not hold Him longer;
Death is strong, but Life is stronger;
Stronger than the dark, the light;
Stronger than the wrong, the right
—Phillips Brooks, "An Easter Carol"

➲ We are Easter people, and hallelujah is our song. This is a week for worship! Start out each day this week in abandoned, joyful praise and worship.

➲ Proclaim the gospel to at least one person this week. Could you imagine your life if you didn't know what Jesus did for us? Don't let others suffer such a fate—share the good news!

➲ Have you been living a life that is anything but a resurrection life? Confess this to God, repent, and commit to being an Easter person. God is faithful to forgive and to help us start again.

[GROUP DISCUSSION]

The following questions are meant to help your group enter into meaningful discussion that we pray will help you become more fully devoted followers of Christ. They are simply a guide, so you don't have to use or get through all of them. You may want to look through them ahead of time and identify the ones that would work well with your group. Any questions you don't get to might be used by your group members for study and reflection in their personal devotional times. And if your group is already comfortable together, feel free to skip the icebreaker question. Remember, it's all about community, so let the Spirit guide your discussion where he wants it to go.

ICE BREAKER

Share about a time when you were part of a life-giving community, inside or outside of the church (this may have been in a family, group of friends, team, organization, etc.). What made this experience so memorable?

Reflections from the Week

Depending on your group size, break into groups of two or three and do or ask the following:

- Have everyone review their notes from their personal study time. Share with one another what you learned from the readings. Are there any questions you'd like to discuss with the group?

- What stood out to you most about Acts 2?

- Were you able to share the gospel with someone this week? If so, share the story with your group.

[**WATCH DVD**] **Session 2**

◗ *Discussion Questions*

Read Acts 2:2–4.

- What role does the Holy Spirit play in fellowship and community?

- How can you experience the power of the Holy Spirit, both individually and as a life group? (Leader: offer to talk more in depth about salvation with any of your group members who may not have experienced the indwelling of the Holy Spirit.)

Read Acts 2:42–47.

- In what ways does your life group currently reflect this model of community?

- Other than wearing masks, what are some factors that keep you from experiencing true community with one another?

- What can your group do practically to become a reflection of true biblical community?

Challenge

What specific action(s) can your group take to build community with one another? For example, look for opportunities to share life together outside of group meetings (social outings, serving in the community, etc.); or look for opportunities to build and share community with others by inviting them to join your life group. Also, as group members share their needs, look for ways that you as a group can rally around each other. Lastly, as the group leader, who can you empower to serve the group by coordinating fun group activities, service projects, or prayer requests?

Close in [PRAYER]

Father, Son, and Holy Spirit, move among us today so that the world may see from our love that we are your followers. Ignite within us a passion for you that cannot be quenched, and open our hearts to receive all the good things you have for us. In your holy name, Amen.

[YOUTH DISCUSSION]

Don't be afraid of being weird. God's power is mysterious and strange, and he invites us to join in by receiving the gift of his Holy Spirit. When the Spirit works through you, you'll make a tremendous difference for the kingdom of God. But people might think you're a little strange for standing out in God's light. Are you willing to receive this gift from God?

THIS SESSION'S [BIG] IDEA

Do I have all that God wishes for me to have?

Memory Verse

All of them were filled with the Holy Spirit and began to speak in other tongues as the Spirit enabled them. (Acts 2.4)

[WATCH DVD] SESSION 2

➲ Discussion Questions

1. Has a relationship with a friend or family member shown you that God is real and he loves you? Have you felt the freedom to open up and be honest?

2. Joy and freedom defined the church from the beginning. Do you feel that's still true today?

3. Do you believe God will accept and love you, issues and all?

4. Can others see that God's love is real when they look at your life?

5. Are you willing to let your guard down, drop your act, take off your mask?

Challenge

Identify one thing you do to pretend you have it all together in your life, and then work on being more real in that area this week.

[FAMILY DISCUSSION]

This week's message: God has amazing gifts for us; are we receiving them?

[LIFEBOOK] Idea of the Week

When the day of Pentecost came, they were all together in one place. Suddenly a sound like the blowing of a violent wind came from heaven and filled the whole house where they were sitting. They saw what seemed to be tongues of fire that separated and came to rest on each of them. All of them were filled with the Holy Spirit and began to speak in other tongues as the Spirit enabled them. (Acts 2:1–4)

Summary

God gave his people the gift of the Holy Spirit at Pentecost. When they received him, they were able to do miracles, speak the gospel message boldly, and speak in tongues. All these gifts helped them to bring new people to Christ. It was an amazing time, but God still has those gifts for us today if we're willing to receive them.

[LIFELINE] The Main Point

Open yourself up to take the gifts God wants to give you.

[LIFEVERSE] Memorize This!

All of them were filled with the Holy Spirit and began to speak in other tongues as the Spirit enabled them. (Acts 2:4)

[LIFECHALLENGE]
Talk together as a family.

1. Do you feel that you can be honest with God and your family about the times you mess up, or do you think you need to pretend as though you are perfectly good all the time?

2. We all make mistakes and sin—how can we know God loves us even though we do this?

3. Who do we know who doesn't know God loves them? How can we share God's love with these friends?

4. Do you feel as though you have all the gifts God wants to give you, or have you been unwilling to receive some of them? (Consider the fruits of the Spirit, the gifts mentioned here, and those mentioned in 1 Corinthians 12–14.)

Action

➲ Talk together about what gifts God has given each member of your family, and identify a way you can use those gifts to glorify God this week.

NOTES

BECOMING WEIGHTLESS

Repent, then, and
turn to God, so that
your sins may be
wiped out, that times
of refreshing may
come from the Lord.

—Acts 3:19

[CONSIDER]
BECOMING WEIGHTLESS

By Billy Hornsby

Acts 3 starts with one of the first big miracles of the early church after Pentecost. As Peter and John were approaching the synagogue for worship, they encountered a man who was begging near the gate where they would enter. Peter and John had no gold or silver to offer him, but they gave him something much more powerful— they healed him of his affliction so he could walk again (v. 6). This beggar wasn't simply trying to skirt responsibility by begging for his income and returning home to a nice hotel and a warm dinner; this man had reached the end of his rope and was honestly seeking help. As soon as he was healed, he was rejoicing and praising God. This was a life-changing moment for him. The burden of his paralysis was gone, and he was free to worship God!

Sometimes, like the beggar, our expectation for the things of this world let us down. In those moments we need to refocus on the person of Christ. No matter how good a businessperson you are, your business can fail. No matter how sweet and kind you are, your relationships can fail. But when we focus on Christ, we are setting the foundation of our lives on something solid we can trust.

The truth is that whatever gets your attention, gets you. And in a world full of distractions, we have to "pay" attention. There's a cost involved—whatever you're giving your attention to will cost you something, and either the price can be worth it or it can be a waste. Make sure you're paying your attention to the things of Christ. Proverbs 4:25–27 reminds us,

> Let your eyes look straight ahead;
>> fix your gaze directly before you.
> Make level paths for your feet
>> and take only ways that are firm.
> Do not swerve to the right or the left;
>> keep your foot from evil.

We've all messed up. We've looked away from our goal, and we've lost track of where we are. Our burdens and regrets are like large stones, and the longer we hold on to them, the heavier they become. God promises deliverance from these burdens when we retrain our focus on Christ.

When NASA's astronauts go out for a space walk, they seem to be weightless, suspended in zero gravity, just floating. We've probably all wondered what would happen to them if they just drifted off, into oblivion. It's a scary thought to be drifting through space with no hope of ever getting back to your mother ship. That's why the astronauts always stay tethered to the shuttle. Like them, we must stay tethered to Jesus. He died so that we could live weightless lives. We can lay our burdens down, and he will take them from us. He will wipe out our sin, and a time of refreshing will come. It is a beautiful gift, and all we have to do is be willing to receive it.

[**READ**]

Jesus Christ had risen from the dead. The disciples had been given their mission and had been filled with the Holy Spirit. And now in Acts 3, we see what these new Spirit-empowered lives looked like. Let's dig in . . .

Begin by reading through the entirety of Acts 3. Commit to reading it through every day this week.

Memory Verse

"By faith in the name of Jesus, this man whom you see and know was made strong. It is Jesus' name and the faith that comes through him that has given this complete healing to him, as you can all see." (Acts 3:16)

---

1. Summarize the events that take place in Acts 3.

2. According to Acts 3:1, what were Peter and John doing? Do you think this was a regular occurrence?

3. What do you learn about the lame man in verse 2?

4. With what power did Peter perform the miracle?

5. What was the man's response upon being healed?

6. What was the reaction of the people who witnessed the miracle?

7. What did Peter then do?

8. According to verses 11–16, where did the credit for the miracle lie?

9. What did Peter say is the result of genuine repentance (verses 19–21)? Compare this to 2 Chronicles 7:14.

10. How are the events in this chapter similar to and different from those in Acts 2?

[**REFLECT**]

- In what area of your life are you in need of healing? How can you apply the events of Acts 3 to your situation?

- How do you typically respond when you come across someone in need of healing? How does your reaction compare to that of Peter and John?

- How can you tell if something you are feeling is from the Holy Spirit or not?

- Do you believe that healing miracles still occur today? Why or why not?

- Would you say that you listen and are watchful for the Holy Spirit's prompting throughout your day?

- Think through some of the good things that happened in the past few days. To whom did you give the credit?

[ACTION STEPS]

⊃ Make sure you are giving God credit for the miracles big and small that occur. Make a practice of praising and thanking him at the end of each day.

⊃ Who do you know who is in need of healing? What can you do this week to bring the name of Jesus into their situation?

⊃ Go an entire day looking each person you come across in the eye. As you do, pray, "Lord, do you have anything you want me to give to this person?" Follow through on however the Holy Spirit prompts you.

⊃ Are you in need of refreshing in your life? Repent, regularly and authentically.

⊃ Share the gospel with at least one person this week.

[GROUP DISCUSSION]

The following questions are meant to help your group enter into meaningful discussion that we pray will help you become more fully devoted followers of Christ. They are simply a guide, so you don't have to use or get through all of them. You may want to look through them ahead of time and identify the ones that would work well with your group. Any questions you don't get to might be used by your group members for study and reflection in their personal devotional times. And if your group is already comfortable together, feel free to skip the icebreaker question. Remember, it's all about community, so let the Spirit guide your discussion where he wants it to go.

ICE **BREAKER**

How do you tend to respond when people ask you for things—money, help, advice, time, and so on?

Reflections from the Week

Depending on your group size, break into groups of two or three and do or ask the following:

• Have everyone review their notes from their personal study time. Share with one another what you learned from the readings. Are there any questions you'd like to discuss with the group?

• Did you see God do any miracles this week? Remember that even the things we consider to be "small" (like having just enough money in the bank or avoiding a car accident) can be miraculous.

• Did you practice looking in the eye each person you encountered this week? How did that go? Were you led to help someone in some specific way?

[WATCH DVD] SESSION 3

➲ *Discussion Questions*

Read Acts 3:1–10.

• What did the lame man ask of Peter and John? What did they give him instead?

• How can we tell when the Holy Spirit is prompting us to act?

Read Acts 3:11–16.

• Share about any Holy Spirit miracles you've witnessed, big or small.

• Where do you currently need a Holy Spirit–type of faith?

• How can you make yourself available for God to use in supernatural ways?

Challenge

Ask and discuss with the group, "Is there an area in which God wants you to exercise faith right now?" Pray as a group that God would help you discern and respond to his will in faith.

Close in [PRAYER]

God, please use us this week to transform our world for your glory. Give us the courage to seek you in everything we do and say, and help us to keep our focus on you so that we don't become distracted by the things of this world. In your holy name, Amen.

[YOUTH DISCUSSION]

Have you done things that you really regret? Maybe you've gossiped about a friend or done something you're ashamed of on a date. In school, there are so many distractions, so many ways to cut corners and forget that God is calling you to greatness. But when we keep our focus on Christ, we'll know that we can take all those burdens and all that regret and just dump it at his feet. He'll make you weightless with the freedom of forgiveness, and you'll be able to make a radical difference for him.

THIS SESSION'S [BIG] IDEA

Focus on Christ, and he will take away the burden of your sin.

Memory Verse

"By faith in the name of Jesus, this man whom you see and know was made strong. It is Jesus' name and the faith that comes through him that has given this complete healing to him, as you can all see." (Acts 3:16)

[WATCH DVD] SESSION 3

○ Discussion Questions

1. How did Peter have the power to heal the man by the temple gate?

2. Does God require us to have a few things in place, to have good works ready, in order to use us? Or could it really be faith alone that changes us?

3. Discuss the illustration with the pieces of wood in the video. What is the significance of the wall between us and God?

4. What are the pieces of the "tower of righteousness" you've tried to build? How can you give those over to God?

5. What will happen when we come to God in faith?

Challenge

Ask God to use you to heal one of his children this week. Be on the lookout for who that might be, and make yourself available to listen to, encourage, pray with, or support that friend, even if it's inconvenient.

[FAMILY DISCUSSION]

This week's message: When we bring our burdens and sins to Christ, he will take them from us and give us freedom!

[LIFEBOOK] Idea of the Week

"By faith in the name of Jesus, this man whom you see and know was made strong. It is Jesus' name and the faith that comes through him that has given this complete healing to him, as you can all see." (Acts 3:16)

Summary

There are tons of distractions in life, and it's important that we focus on Christ so we'll always know we're on track. We have to ask ourselves: "Will I be on God's team, or will I choose a worthless life?" When we join God's team, he promises to take away all our burdens and all our fears, and replace them with the feeling that we're flying, weightless, with his freedom and joy.

[LIFELINE] The Main Point

Take your burdens to Christ, and he will make you free.

[LIFEVERSE] **Memorize This!**

By faith in the name of Jesus, this man whom you see and know was made strong. (Acts 3:16)

[LIFECHALLENGE]
Talk together as a family.

1. How did the man react after he was healed?

2. When you have had problems solved in your life, have you responded the way the man did in the story?

3. The Bible says that Peter and John healed by faith. Do you think God still uses his people today to heal others? (Think of all the ways you might be "healed.")

4. What does Jesus want from you in order to use you for his glory? (Do you need to "have it all together," or do you just need to come to him?)

Action

○ Sit at the dinner table together, and have each person write down one thing on a private piece of paper that has been a burden to him or her—maybe something he or she has worried about, been afraid of, or felt badly about. You can choose to share them if you like. When you're finished, pray together for Christ to take these burdens; then destroy your papers as a symbol of you giving them to him.

NOTES

ONE EXTRAORDINARY PRAYER

But Peter and John replied, "Judge for yourselves whether it is right in God's sight to obey you rather than God. For we cannot help speaking about what we have seen and heard."

—Acts 4:19–20

[CONSIDER]
ONE EXTRAORDINARY PRAYER
By Greg Surratt

Shortly after Peter and John healed the crippled man near the temple, they were arrested for doing this marvelous act *in Jesus' name.* It had just been a few weeks since these very same religious leaders had crucified Jesus, and now Peter and John found themselves in jail—possibly the same cell in which Jesus had been thrown—and preparing to stand before the same men who put Jesus on trial.

The high priest challenged the men, asking in whose name they were doing these wonders. They did not cower. Peter was filled with the Holy Spirit, and he boldly told them that they were living in service to Jesus Christ, whom the religious leaders had crucified.

The leaders were outraged and ordered Peter and John to not speak Jesus' name again, upon threat of death. Since all business transactions went through the temple, being outcast like this would mean certain poverty and severe hardship for these men and their families. How they responded would be a real test of their faith.

They returned to the fellowship of believers, and they committed immediately to pray over this development. And while their prayer is enlightening, it's what they didn't pray for that is very striking. Although they were in imminent danger, these men did not pray for safety. They didn't ask for comfort or even victory or revenge. They knew that God would win the ultimate battle, and their focus wasn't on this life—it was on eternity and God's kingdom.

So they prayed for boldness. They asked for healing and signs and wonders. They asked the Lord to let them live such extraordinary lives that the only explanation would be the power of God in them.

The house began to shake, and the Holy Spirit filled these people. They were granted everything they asked for—boldness, unity, generosity, power, and grace. They were passionate about their mission, and God gave them extraordinary lives of faith. So, what's your prayer today?

NOTES

[READ]

In Acts 4, the disciples learned firsthand that completing the mission Jesus gave them wouldn't be smooth sailing, as they were brought before the very men who had crucified Jesus just months before. Let's dig in and see what we can learn about Spirit-empowered boldness in the life of a Christ-follower.

Begin by reading through the entirety of Acts 4. Commit to reading it through every day this week.

Memory Verse

But Peter and John replied, "Judge for yourselves whether it is right in God's sight to obey you rather than God. For we cannot help speaking about what we have seen and heard." (Acts 4:19–20)

1. Glance back at Acts 3. What had just occurred prior to the events of chapter 4?

2. Why were Peter and John arrested?

3. According to Acts 4:5–6, who gathered to try Peter and John?

4. What do you learn about these men and their role in Jesus' crucifixion in John 18?

5. Peter could have backed down in fear. Instead, how did he respond to their inquiry in Acts 4:7–12?

6. What do you think enabled Peter and John to respond this way? See verses 8 and 20 for clues.

7. Once Peter and John were released, the believers gathered to pray. Instead of praying for their safety, what did the believers pray for?

8. Why do you think they were able to pray this way?

9. Slowly read through the believers' prayer in verses 24–30. On which attributes of God did they focus?

10. Reread verses 32–37, the description of the community of believers. What do you think caused this unity?

[REFLECT]

- Reread Acts 4:13. Would someone observing your life be able to tell that you have the Holy Spirit within you?

- In Acts 4:14, we see that the rulers and elders had nothing to say in opposition to Peter and James, because the man they had healed was standing right next to them. What evidence can you point to in your life that shows the truth of the gospel?

- What, if anything, is your biggest hindrance to sharing the gospel with others?

- Would you say that you pray more for deliverance from problems or for the boldness to face them head-on? Why do you think this is?

- In what ways has your experience with Christian community been similar to or different from that described in Acts 4?

[ACTION STEPS]

⟲ This week, practice praying for boldness. Model your prayers after that of the believers in Acts 4:24–30.

⟲ There is something powerful about praying with other Christians. Commit to praying together with a group of other believers at least once a week.

⟲ If you are not already doing so, pray for Christians around the world who are being persecuted because of the gospel. Check out the Voice of the Martyrs website for more information (www.persecution.com).

Resources

• Suggested reading: Mark Batterson's *Wild Goose Chase.*

• Watch the message "Powerful Like Jesus" at www.seacoast .org/?p=832 for more information on being filled with the Holy Spirit.

[GROUP DISCUSSION]

The following questions are meant to help your group enter into meaningful discussion that we pray will help you become more fully devoted followers of Christ. They are simply a guide, so you don't have to use or get through all of them. You may want to look through them ahead of time and identify the ones that would work well with your group. Any questions you don't get to might be used by your group members for study and reflection in their personal devotional times. And if your group is already comfortable together, feel free to skip the icebreaker question. Remember, it's all about community, so let the Spirit guide your discussion where he wants it to go.

 **BREAKER**

What is your initial reaction when things don't go according to plan? Why do you think you typically respond that way?

Reflections from the Week

Depending on your group size, break into groups of two or three and share the following:

- Have everyone review their notes from their personal study time. Share with one another what you learned from the readings. Are there any questions you'd like to discuss with the group?

- Have any of you ever been scorned or ridiculed for your faith? How did you handle the situation?

[] Session 4

➲ *Discussion Questions*

Read Acts 4:1–22.

- Do you ever feel as though God has let you down? If so, in what ways?

- What do you do in these circumstances?

- Share with your life group some of the ways God has come through for you in the past.

Read Acts 4:23–31.

- Even though the disciples had just been persecuted, what did they pray for?

- What would you say the majority of your prayer life is focused upon?

- What might this reveal about your faith or your relationship with God?

- Where do you currently need boldness from God in your life?

Challenge

Pray a prayer of boldness, modeled after Acts 4:23–30. After taking prayer requests from your members, thank God for who he is, and give each situation to him, asking that he would fill each of you with the Holy Spirit so that you can continue living out the mission to which he has called you. Go forward in faith that God is for you and will be with you!

Close in [PRAYER]

Heavenly Father, enable us as your servants to speak your Word with great boldness. Stretch out your hand to heal and perform signs and wonders through the name of your Son, Jesus Christ. Amen.

[YOUTH DISCUSSION]

What kind of life do you want to live? Do you want to be normal and ordinary, or do you want God to use you to do amazing things? If you're willing, God will fill you with his Holy Spirit and use you to change the world. Are you ready for that kind of adventure?

THIS SESSION'S [BIG] IDEA

With the Holy Spirit in us, we can live extraordinary lives that are only explained by the power of God in us.

Memory Verse

But Peter and John replied, "Judge for yourselves whether it is right in God's sight to obey you rather than God. For we cannot help speaking about what we have seen and heard." (Acts 4:19–20)

[] SESSION 4

➲ *Discussion Questions*

1. Do you feel God has ever let you down?

2. What prayers has God answered for you?

3. When you face persecution, what do you usually pray to God?

4. How do you think the disciples' prayer could change things today?

Challenge

Look back over your life, and make a record of all the times you can recall when God has been there for you during a difficult situation.

[FAMILY DISCUSSION]

This week's message: God wants us to live extraordinary lives for his glory.

[LIFEBOOK] Idea of the Week

But Peter and John replied, "Judge for yourselves whether it is right in God's sight to obey you rather than God. For we cannot help speaking about what we have seen and heard." (Acts 4:19–20)

Summary

When the disciples faced hard persecution for their faith, they prayed for more boldness and the ability to share God's good news even more. They weren't scared for their own safety—their focus was on God's kingdom. That's how they were able to live extraordinary lives.

[LIFELINE] The Main Point

Ask God for boldness, and he'll give you the faith you need to live an extraordinary life through the power of the Holy Spirit.

[LIFEVERSE] Memorize This!

But Peter and John replied, "Judge for yourselves whether it is right in God's sight to obey you rather than God. For we cannot help speaking about what we have seen and heard." (Acts 4:19–20)

[LIFECHALLENGE]
Talk together as a family.

1. How do you think God might want to use your life, and our family, to do great things in his name?

2. Have you ever felt persecuted because you believe in Jesus?

3. Tell about a time when you asked God for help, and he came to your rescue.

4. Who do you want to tell about the good things God has done?

Action

⮕ The disciples were marked by generosity, among other things. Discuss a way your family can open up your home or share your resources to help spread the good news of God's love with those who haven't heard it before.

NOTES

THE RIPPLE EFFECT

Then Peter said,
"Ananias, how is
it that Satan has
so filled your heart
that you have lied to
the Holy Spirit . . . ?
You have not lied to
men but to God."

—Acts 5:3–4

[CONSIDER]
THE RIPPLE EFFECT

By Greg Surratt

When a stone hits the surface of the water in a pond, a ripple effect immediately takes place. The concentric rings spread out to the far stretches of the body of water, and underneath the surface, as the pebble drops through the water, fish scatter and plants sway. Our actions have effects—sometimes positive ones and sometimes negative.

Back in Acts, the church was just starting to really get going. They'd asked for boldness, and they were living in great unity and community. But when the first stone was dropped in that peaceful pool and the waves started to expand outward, the people were shocked to see how God would respond.

The members of the early church had been overwhelmed with generosity, and many were giving everything they had to the movement. It was the result of God's love bursting from inside of them, not something mandated by church leaders. So when one of the couples who had become involved sold some land, they felt they should give the money to the church. The problem was, they didn't really want to. So out of obligation and a desire to look the part, they came to Peter and told him that they were donating all the money from the sale of the land. But Peter was filled with the

Holy Spirit, and he knew a lie as soon as he heard it. He confronted Ananias, who fell dead on the spot. A little while later Ananias's wife, Sapphira, came in to corroborate the story, and she also died.

Pride mixed with competition can be a deadly recipe for any ministry that's getting started, and God knew it could be the end of the early church if those ripples continued to grow. So he stopped them immediately and clearly. Scripture tells us that the people were afraid (Acts 5:5, 11). They took God seriously, as these events created a high degree of accountability among their community. Honesty swept through their church as they recognized how seriously God takes selfish exaggeration and pompous lies.

When sin spreads through a community, it short-circuits the work of the Holy Spirit in our lives. And when we have been cut off from our Source, the work of the Holy Spirit cannot move forward in our community either. God's desire is for us to be unified, to work together to promote his kingdom throughout the world (Eph. 4:3). So we must take sin seriously. If you have the ability to save someone who is drowning, save him! Likewise, if you have a friend who is dying in her sin, lovingly confront her. And quickly forgive. Without this healing, your community will become paralyzed in inaction. So let your ripple effect be one of love, honesty, and forgiveness. With regular repentance, God can use you to do wonderful things for his kingdom.

[READ]

In Acts 5, we move from the exciting description of the unity of the church to the sobering and cautionary tale of Ananias and Sapphira. Let's dig in and see what we can learn about God's kingdom and about his heart for the church.

Be sure to watch the message "Powerful Like Jesus" for further study on being filled with the Holy Spirit. (This can be found online at http://www.seacoast.org/?p=832.)

Read through Acts 5. Though we will mostly be focusing on the story of Ananias and Sapphira, you may want to commit to reading all of Acts 5 each day this week, trusting that God will open your eyes to what he has to teach you through his Word.

Memory Verse

Then Peter said, "Ananias, how is it that Satan has so filled your heart that you have lied to the Holy Spirit . . . ? You have not lied to men but to God." (Acts 5:3–4)

---

1. Reread Acts 4:32–37. According to this passage, what types of things characterized the church at this time?

2. Contrast the actions of Joseph/Barnabas in 4:34–37 to those of Ananias and Sapphira.

3. What clues does this passage give you that suggest there was a spiritual battle happening behind Ananias and Sapphira's decision?

4. Why do you think God pronounced such immediate and severe judgment? What scriptural evidence can you find that supports your answer?

5. One theory about God's judgment in this passage is that he wanted to protect the purity and integrity of his church during this important period of growth. If we don't understand the importance of the church, we will never understand or trust God's judgment. Read the following passages. What do they teach you about the body of Christ? What do they tell you about God's heart for his church?

- Matthew 16:18

- Acts 20:28

- 1 Corinthians 12:14–31

- Ephesians 5:22–33

[REFLECT]

- How do you respond to God's judgment in the story of Ananias and Sapphira?

- How do you think your personal choices might be affecting the church as a whole, either in its unity or in its witness to the world?

- Would you say that you value the church as highly as God does? Why or why not?

- What selfishness or individualism do you need to sacrifice for the sake of the church?

- How do you respond when someone confronts you about your sin?

- When did you feel most filled with the Spirit?

- When did you feel the least Spirit-filled?

[ACTION STEPS]

⮑ Be sure you are taking your sin seriously. Each evening, repent of any sin. Ask yourself, "Who has my sin affected?" Ask for forgiveness this week.

⮑ Is there anyone whose behavior you need to confront? Do so this week in love and grace.

⮑ Start out each day this week in prayer. Ask God to fill you with the Holy Spirit to enable you to live boldly throughout the day.

⮑ Consider reading the classic book *Life Together* by Dietrich Bonhoeffer.

[GROUP DISCUSSION]

The following questions are meant to help your group enter into meaningful discussion that we pray will help you become more fully devoted followers of Christ. They are simply a guide, so you don't have to use or get through all of them. You may want to look through them ahead of time and identify the ones that would work well with your group. Any questions you don't get to might be used by your group members for study and reflection in their personal devotional times. And if your group is already comfortable together, feel free to skip the icebreaker question. Remember, it's all about community, so let the Spirit guide your discussion where he wants it to go.

ICE BREAKER

When was the last time you admitted you were wrong? Is that hard for you to do? Why or why not?

Reflections from the Week

Depending on your group size, break into groups of two or three and do or ask the following:

- Have everyone review their notes from their personal study time. Share with one another what you learned from the readings. Are there any questions you'd like to discuss with the group?

- What was your initial reaction to the story of Ananias and Sapphira? What could they have done differently?

- When was a time you felt the Holy Spirit really working through you? When was a time you felt you were acting out of your own flesh rather than following the Spirit's lead?

[WATCH DVD] SESSION 5

⊃ *Discussion Questions*

Read Acts 5:1–11. God's judgment in this situation may appear severe.

- Why do you think it was necessary? What was the result?

- What do you learn about the character of God from this story?

- What does it mean to fear the Lord?

- Why do you think people are so inclined to lie?

- In what ways does this type of deceit play out among Christians and in the church?

Read Proverbs 1:7.

- How can you develop a healthy fear of God in your life?

Challenge

Ask everyone to think about one person with whom they can share their struggles and confess their sins, as it says in James 5:16. Pray as a group that God would provide the right person for each of you and that he will equip each of you to be the same kind of individual to someone else. Challenge everyone in the group to get serious about sin in their lives. As a group, ask God to search your hearts this week and reveal anything that is displeasing to him.

Close in [PRAYER]

Father, you are full of mercy and grace. We thank you for the forgiveness of our sins, which we do not deserve. Help us to be gentle with those we love, but to speak your truth into their lives when necessary. And give us the tenderness to receive your admonition from your children with humility and repentance.

[YOUTH DISCUSSION]

When the church was just getting started, the people were filled with the Holy Spirit and living in a great community. But sin in the form of pride and competition (and lies) entered the picture, and God decided to put an immediate stop to it.

THIS SESSION'S [BIG] IDEA

God takes our sin very seriously.

Memory Verse

Then Peter said, "Ananias, how is it that Satan has so filled your heart that you have lied to the Holy Spirit . . . ? You have not lied to men but to God." (Acts 5:3–4)

 **SESSION 5**

➲ *Discussion Questions*

  1. Have you ever lied to make yourself look better?

2. Sin quenches the Holy Spirit from acting in our lives and relationships. How have you seen this in your life?

3. Do you think God's punishment for Ananias and Sapphira was harsh?

4. Why did God act so severely in this situation?

5. How would your world be different if the people in it got serious about repenting of their sin?

Challenge

Ask God to reveal your sin to you this week, and do what it takes to repent of it. If it means you need to ask forgiveness, restore something that was broken or stolen, or serve in humility, then do so this week.

[FAMILY DISCUSSION]

This week's message: Sin is a serious thing, and God won't allow it to be a part of his community.

[LIFEBOOK] Idea of the Week

Then Peter said, "Ananias, how is it that Satan has so filled your heart that you have lied to the Holy Spirit . . . ? What made you think of doing such a thing? You have not lied to men but to God." (Acts 5:3–4)

Summary

When people in the church lied about how good they were, God saw through it. He immediately stopped the sin so that it wouldn't spread to the other people in the community. When sin starts to get comfortable for us, God's work stops and our own agendas take over instead.

[LIFELINE] The Main Point

Sin destroys relationships, and God hates that.

[LIFEVERSE] Memorize This!

Then Peter said, "Ananias, how is it that Satan has so filled your heart that you have lied to the Holy Spirit . . . ? You have not lied to men but to God." (Acts 5:3–4)

[LIFECHALLENGE]
Talk together as a family.

1. Why is sin such a big deal to God if he is able to forgive us?

2. How does sin mess up relationships?

3. What can we do to be filled with the Holy Spirit instead of sin?

4. What is a good way for us to regularly ask each other for forgiveness?

Action

⮐ Discuss a good plan for your family to have open lines of communication with one another. Perhaps establish a regular family meeting where everyone can feel safe expressing their hurts or desires for the family. Let it be a way for you to focus on being filled with God's Spirit as a family, rather than keeping secrets and trying to pretend you're doing better than you really are.

NOTES

OUTLAST THE GROWING PAINS

But as the believers
rapidly multiplied,
there were rumblings
of discontent.

—Acts 6:1 NLT

[CONSIDER]

OUTLAST THE GROWING PAINS

By Greg Surratt

When the rumblings of discontent begin between just a few, it can threaten your entire community. Usually we're being picky about inconsequential details, but even when the disagreements are about important issues, they still divide believers. And God is calling us to unity.

There are two main threats to unity in the body of Christ: disorganization and distraction. In Acts 6, believers were concerned about the ways the church was taking care of the widows and orphans—those people who depended on the church for their welfare. It was an important issue, and their lack of organization threatened to divide the church.

When the apostles heard the concern, they immediately recognized that it was an issue they hadn't been focusing on, mainly because they knew their focus was to be preaching and teaching the Word of God. The "soup kitchen," while an important ministry of the body of Christ, was not meant to be their responsibility. So, they took action to resolve the issue and preserve the fellowship of believers. The principles we see in their actions are ones we can apply to our conflicts today.

First, they saw the crisis as an opportunity to become better people. They didn't wallow in complaints or fear change—they saw this as an area for potential growth. And that's exactly what it ended up being for them.

Second, they knew that they needed to spend their time doing what they were good at and what they were called to do. God has exciting plans for his kingdom, and he has given his vision and an assignment to each and every one of us. Sometimes it makes sense to join up in partnership with someone whose calling is different from ours; other times our job is to support from the sidelines and let other people serve God in their own ways.

Third, they chose the right people to tackle the problem. These men weren't necessarily experts on the issue, but they were part of the community and were passionate about serving God. They were men who were known to be full of the Spirit, wise, and of impeccable character. They could be trusted, and the apostles put the project into their capable hands.

Fourth, the apostles trusted the team to come up with a solution. They didn't micromanage. Once they put the team in charge, they allowed them to come up with a solution that would serve the widows and orphans and would honor God.

As a result of this conflict resolution, many came to know God. Even some hard cases—like Jewish priests! If we see every challenge we face as a chance to grow, God will amaze us with the opportunities he provides us.

[**READ**]

In Acts 5, we saw how sin threatened the church. Now in Acts 6, we see two more threats: disunity and distraction. Up until now, most of the focus had been on the mission to those outside the church. But at this point the church had grown so much that attention needed to be given to keeping it unified and organized so it could continue to fulfill its calling. Let's dig in and see what the apostles' decision teaches us about the church.

Memory Verse

So the word of God spread. The number of disciples in Jerusalem increased rapidly, and a large number of priests became obedient to the faith. (Acts 6:7)

---

1. Read through Acts 6 each day this week, trusting that God will open your eyes to what he has for you. Sum up the events that take place in this passage:

   • What was the problem facing the church?

   • What was the process for solving the problem?

• What was the solution?

• According to verse 7, what was the result of their solution?

2. In Acts 5, we saw how sin threatened the church. Now, we see two more threats: disunity and distraction. God has a purpose for his church, and both disunity and distraction can stand in the way of this purpose. Read the following verses. Why are unity and focus so important for the church? How can we make sure we stay unified and focused?

Mission
Acts 20:24
Romans 12:1–8
1 Corinthians 12:4–11
Philippians 3:7–16
1 Timothy 4:6–16

Unity
John 17:20–23
1 Corinthians 1:10
1 Corinthians 12:12–20
Ephesians 2:18–22
Ephesians 4:1–6

[**REFLECT**]

- The apostles were able to stay focused because they knew what their mission was. Do you know what yours is? If so, describe it. If not, write out a prayer to God asking him to make your mission clear.

- What things tend to distract you from what you feel God has called you to do?

- In what ways do you think the church is threatened by distraction and disunity today?

- The apostles needed others to step up so they could continue to focus on their mission. Are you doing your part for the church? In what ways?

- Would you say you are more likely to serve the church, or to expect the church to serve you? Why do you think this is?

- Would you be ready if God asked you to step up? The men the apostles chose were described as reputable, full of the Spirit, and full of wisdom (Acts 6:3). What do you need to do to be ready to be used?

[ACTION STEPS]

⮕ Be ready when God calls your name. Work on your character, your spiritual maturity, and your practical skills.

⮕ Stop expecting the church to serve you. Get off the bench, and start serving in your church.

[GROUP DISCUSSION]

The following questions are meant to help your group enter into meaningful discussion that we pray will help you become more fully devoted followers of Christ. They are simply a guide, so you don't have to use or get through all of them. You may want to look through them ahead of time and identify the ones that would work well with your group. Any questions you don't get to might be used by your group members for study and reflection in their personal devotional times. And if your group is already comfortable together, feel free to skip the icebreaker question. Remember, it's all about community, so let the Spirit guide your discussion where he wants it to go.

 **BREAKER**

> Who are some of the people who have had an impact on your relationship with God?

Reflections from the Week

Depending on your group size, break into groups of two or three and do or ask the following:

• Have everyone review their notes from their personal study time. Share with one another what you learned from the readings. Are there any questions you'd like to discuss with the group?

• What are your spiritual gifts? How are you using them in your church? How are you using them in your community?

[WATCH DVD] SESSION 6

⊃ *Discussion Questions*

Read Acts 6.

• Why is it so important for each follower of Christ to be looking for opportunities to serve?

• Stephen, who started out "waiting tables," became the first martyr for the gospel of Jesus Christ. What sacrifices would you be willing to make to share your faith?

Read Philippians 2:1–11.

- How is Jesus our example of true service?

- How can you begin to impact your church with this model of servanthood? Your community? The world?

- Who is one person whom you feel God wants you to impact?

Challenge

Spend extended time this week praying for a mission. Once God reveals it to you, write out a mission statement and post it somewhere prominent so you can stay focused each day.

Close in [PRAYER]

Dear Lord, give us a renewed commitment to be faithful in the "small things" and trust you with the results. Give us wisdom and character, and fill us with your Holy Spirit as we work side by side to spread your good news throughout the world.

[YOUTH DISCUSSION]

If we are faithful in the small things where God asks us to serve, we can have a big impact for his kingdom. So live by faith, trusting that God has you where he wants you. And work together with other believers to create unity and harmony in the kingdom of God.

THIS SESSION'S [BIG] IDEA

Be faithful in the little things and you can help change the world.

Memory Verse

So the word of God spread. The number of disciples in Jerusalem increased rapidly, and a large number of priests became obedient to the faith. (Acts 6:7)

[WATCH DVD] SESSION 6

⮑ *Discussion Questions*

1. What is a "small thing" God is asking you to be faithful in?

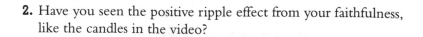

2. Have you seen the positive ripple effect from your faithfulness, like the candles in the video?

3. What is your role in the kingdom of God?

4. Who will you talk to about God's love this week?

Challenge

Pray for God to show you where he wants you to serve, and ask him for the courage to be faithful in that job. Or if you feel you know where he's calling you, look for a practical way to serve in that area this week.

[FAMILY DISCUSSION]

This week's message: Be faithful in the little things and you can change the world.

[LIFEBOOK] Idea of the Week

But as the believers rapidly multiplied, there were rumblings of discontent. (Acts 6:1 NLT)

Summary

There are many ways to serve in the church, and God wants us to work together in unity to spread the good news about him. You might be surprised how many people can be affected when we are faithful to God in the small jobs he gives us.

[LIFELINE] The Main Point

It just takes one person to make a difference for God, and that person can be you!

[LIFEVERSE] Memorize This!

So the word of God spread. The number of disciples in Jerusalem increased rapidly, and a large number of priests became obedient to the faith. (Acts 6:7)

[LIFECHALLENGE]

Talk together as a family.

1. What does it mean that "it starts with one"?

2. Does God want us to help serve the church? How?

3. The men who served God in Acts had character and wisdom, and were full of the Holy Spirit. How can we grow in these characteristics?

4. Who will you tell about God's love this week?

Action

➲ Talk as a family about where God wants you to serve. Make phone calls or talk to people at church or in your community *this week* about what you want to do. Aim to be actively serving in some way within a month.

NOTES

NOTES

[ABOUT THE AUTHORS]

Seacoast Church

Seacoast Church is one of the fastest-growing and most influential churches in the Southeast, with weekend attendance of nearly 11,000 spread over thirteen campuses in three states (North Carolina, South Carolina, Georgia) and on the Internet.

Greg Surratt

Greg is a founding pastor of Seacoast Church and also a founding board member of the Association of Related Churches (ARC), a church-planting network that has given birth to more than 200 churches in the last ten years.

Geoff Surratt

Geoff is the pastor of church planting at Saddleback Church. While on staff at Seacoast Church, Geoff oversaw Seacoast's expansion from one to thirteen locations across three states and from 3,000 to more than 10,000 weekend attendees. He works with other churches across the country in strategic planning and staff development and has also helped train leaders in Europe, Asia, and Africa. He has written the following books: *Ten Stupid Things That Keep Churches from Growing*; *The Multisite Church Revolution*; and *A Multisite Church Roadtrip*.

Billy Hornsby

The late Billy Hornsby was married for more than forty years to his wife, Charlene. As president of ARC, he was a keynote speaker for churches, conferences, and business groups, speaking on the topics of team management, leadership, and how to maintain productive relationships. As a minister he worked for more than thirty years with church leaders nationally and internationally. He was a published author and served as the senior European consultant for EQUIP, John Maxwell's global leadership training organization.